SKATEBOARD DESIGN SKETCHBOOK ONE

CREATE YOUR OWN SKATEBOARD DESIGNS

USE **THIS** BOOK **T**O **C**REATE DESIGNS FOR THE SKATEBOARDS OF **YOUR** DREAM**S.**

Skateboard Design Sketchbook One
©2019 Surf Skate Collective

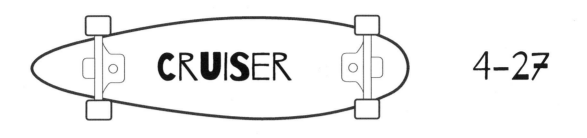 CRUISER 4-27

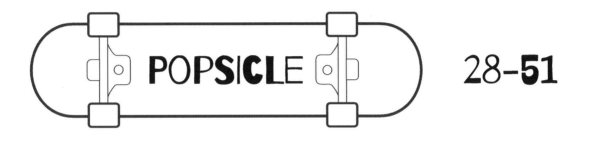 POPSICLE 28-51

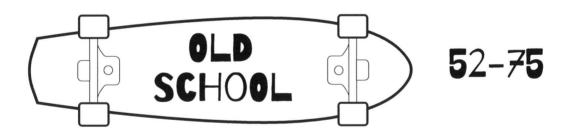 OLD SCHOOL 52-75

 LONGBOARD 76-99

NAME OF BOARD:

DETAILS:

INSPIRATION:

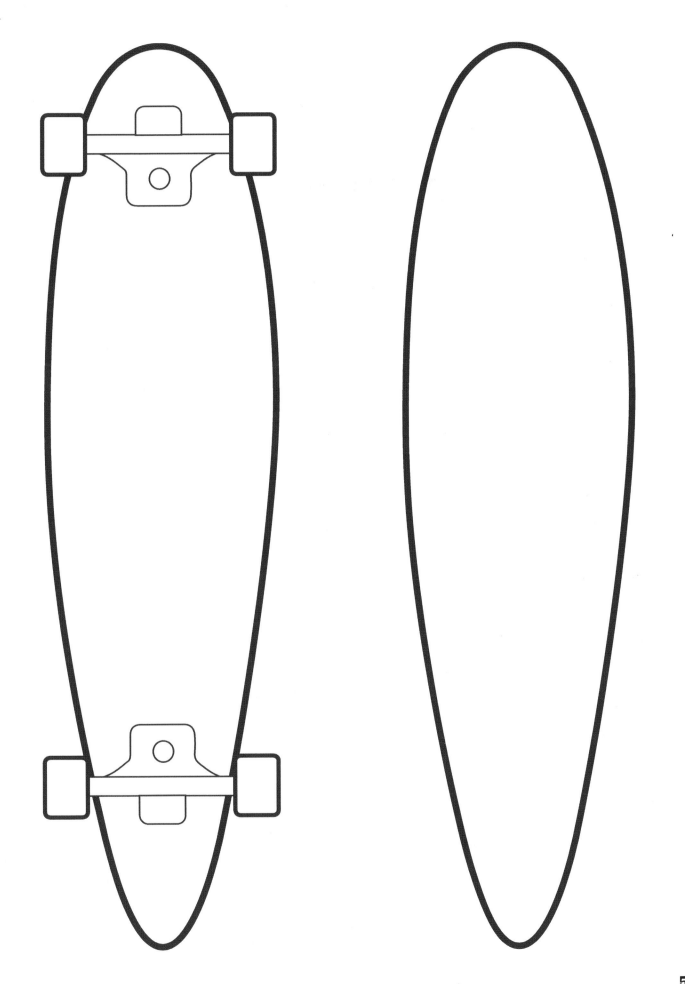

NAME OF BOARD:

DETAILS:

INSPIRATION:

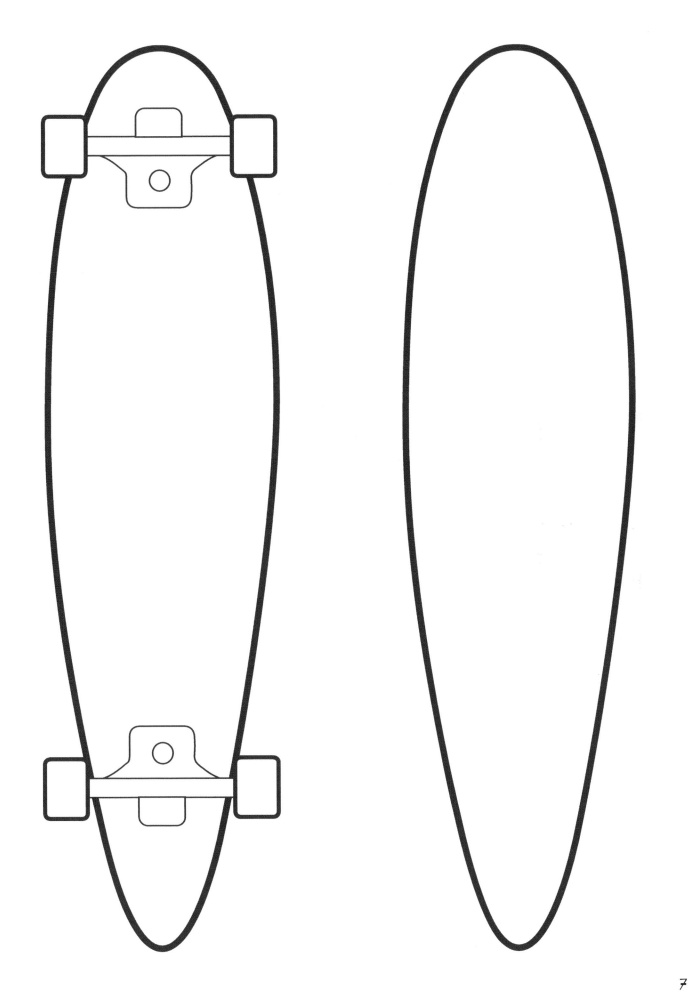

NAME OF BOARD:

DETAILS:

INSPIRATION:

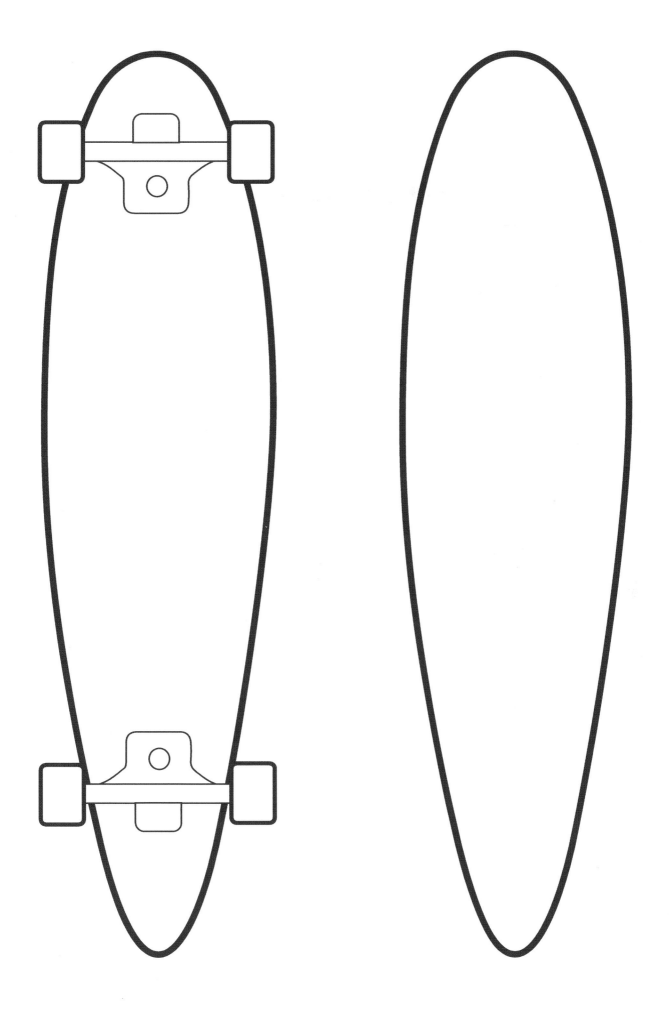

NAME OF BOARD:

DETAILS:

INSPIRATION:

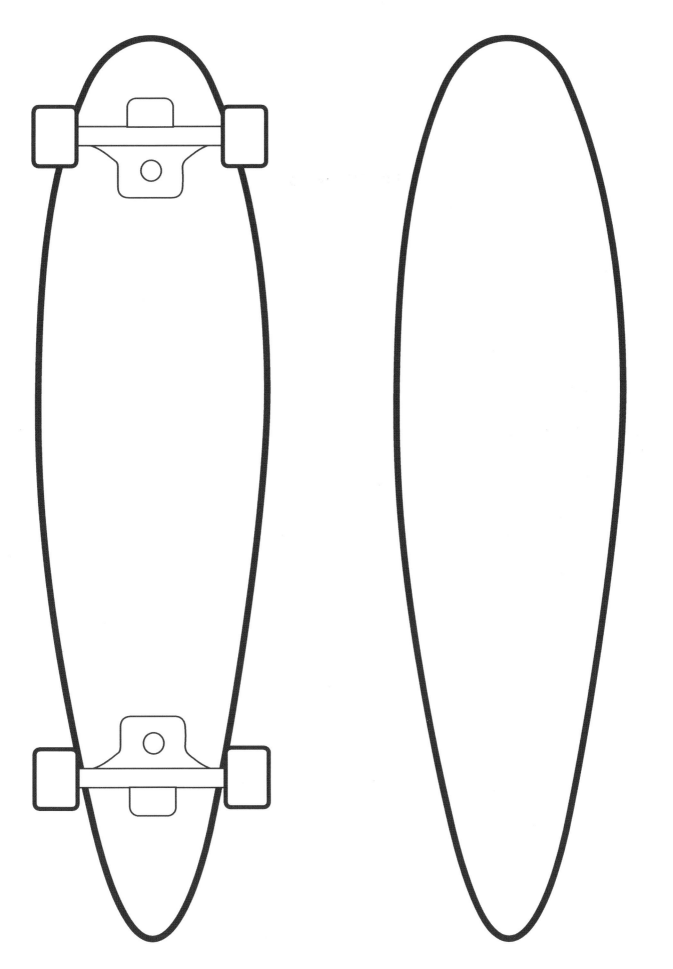

NAME OF BOARD:

DETAILS:

INSPIRATION:

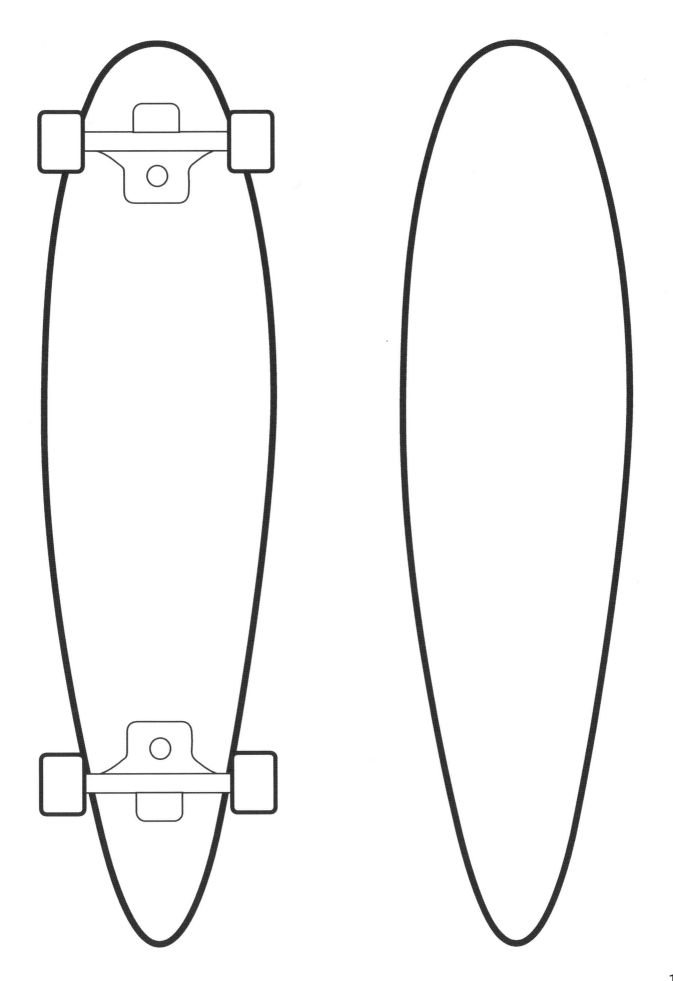

NAME OF BOARD:

DETAILS:

INSPIRATION:

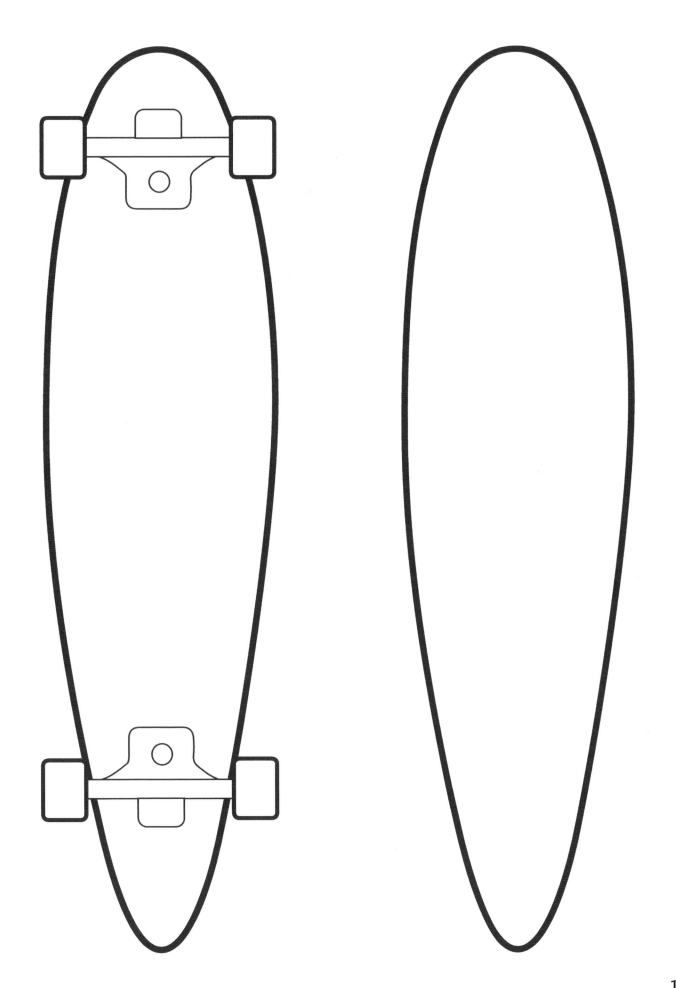

NAME OF BOARD:

DETAILS:

INSPIRATION:

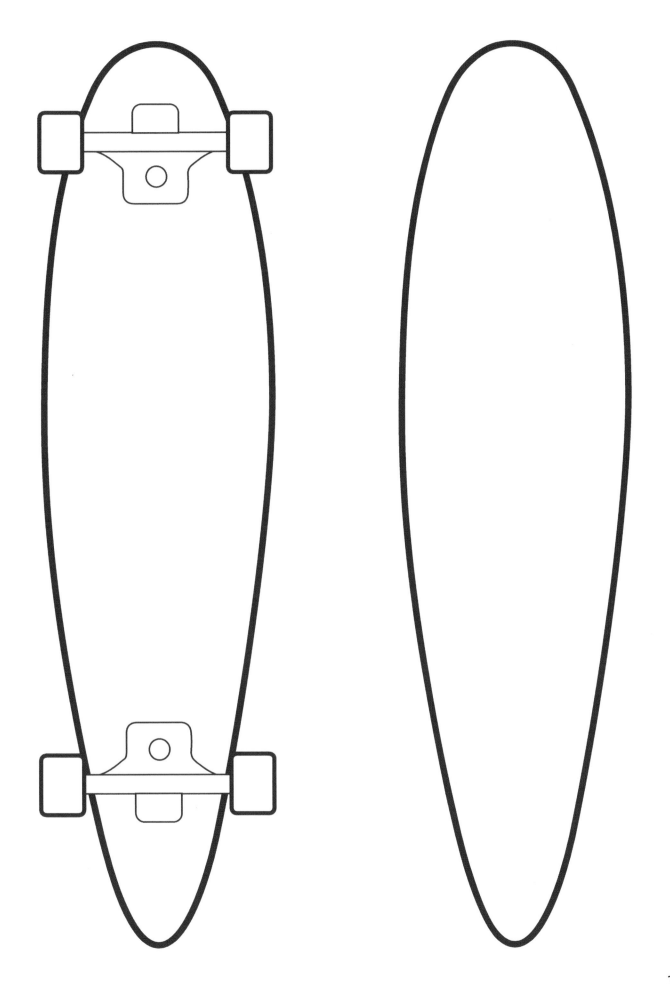

NAME OF BOARD:

DETAILS:

INSPIRATION:

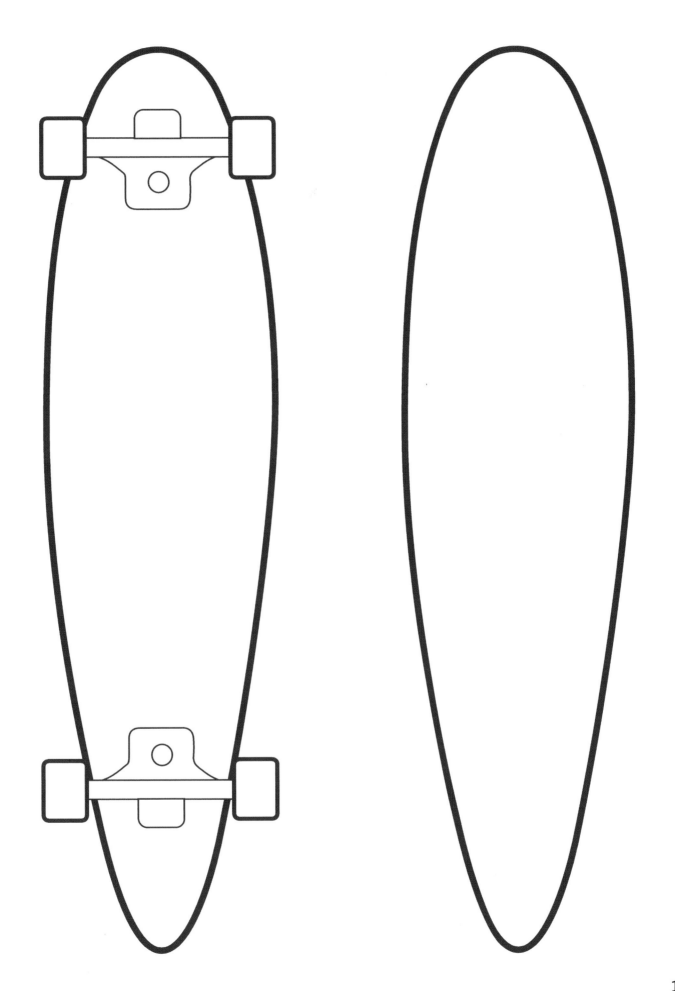

NAME OF BOARD:

DETAILS:

INSPIRATION:

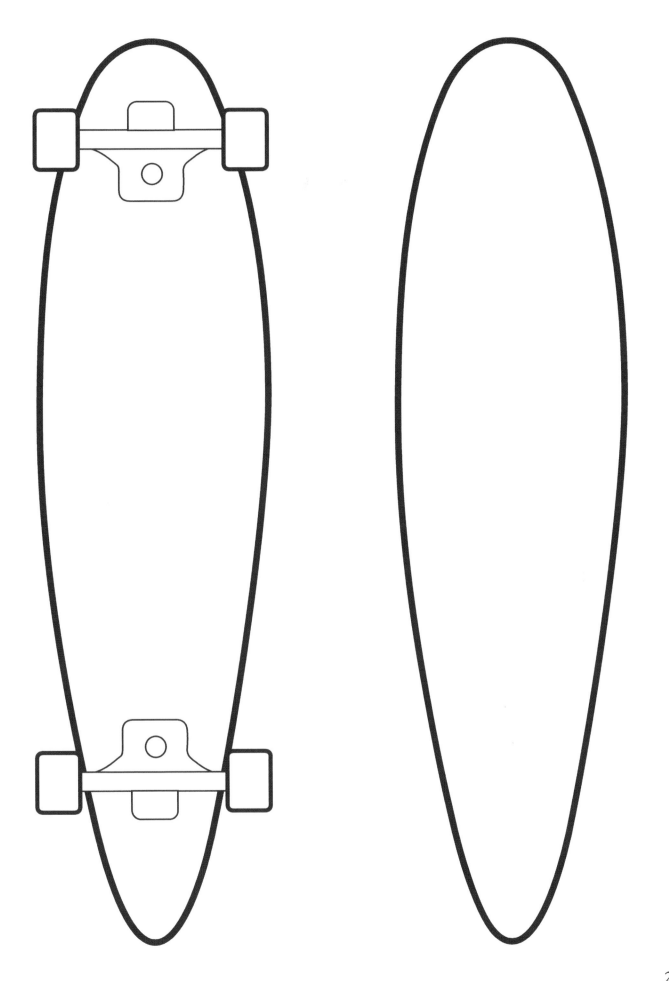

NAME OF BOARD:

DETAILS:

INSPIRATION:

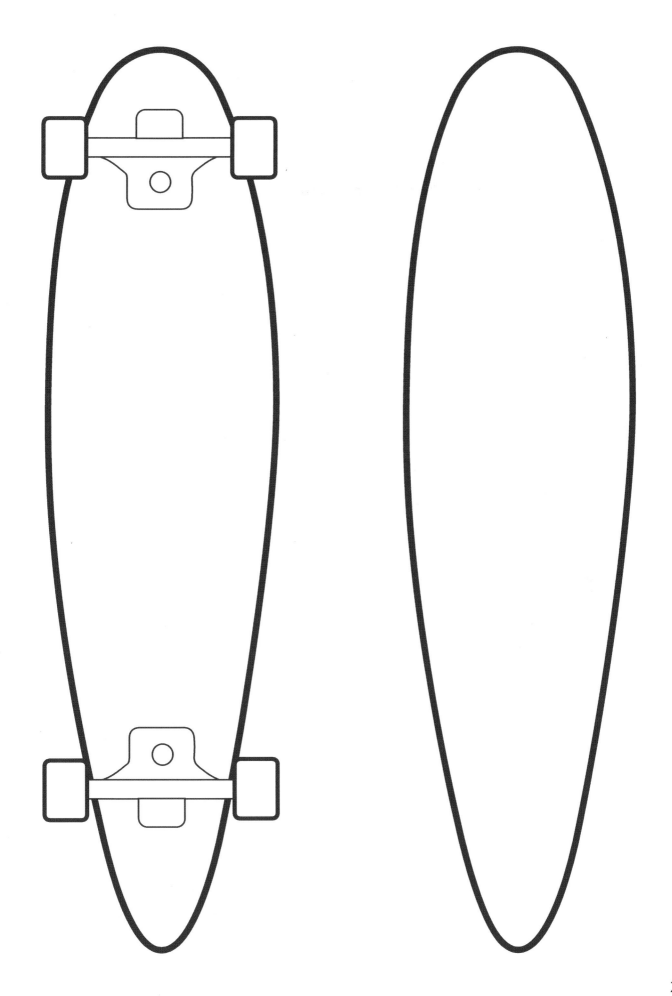

NAME OF BOARD:

DETAILS:

INSPIRATION:

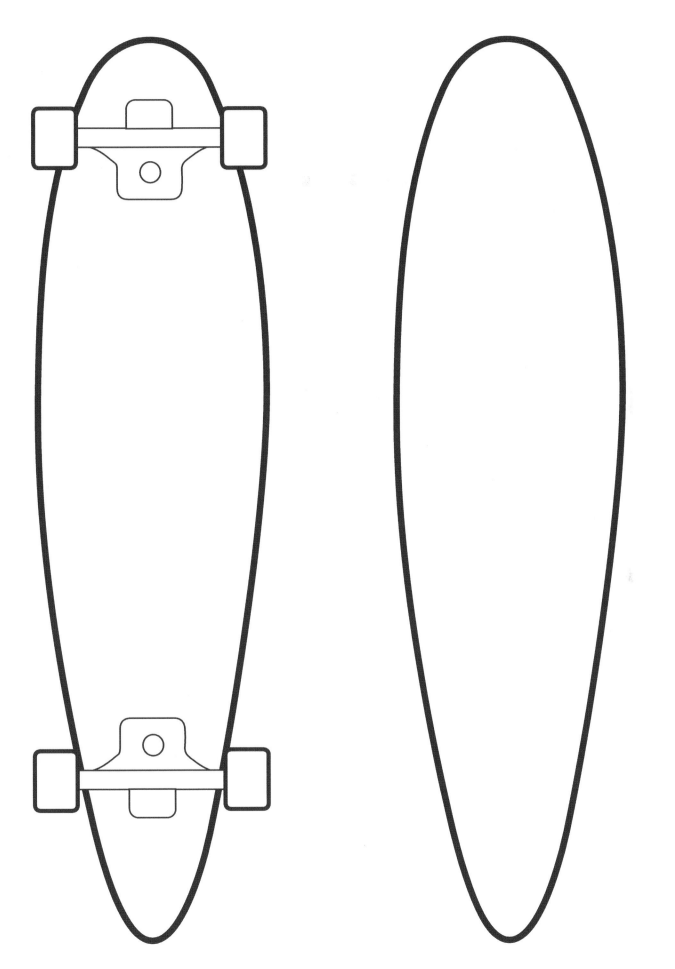

NAME OF BOARD:

DETAILS:

INSPIRATION:

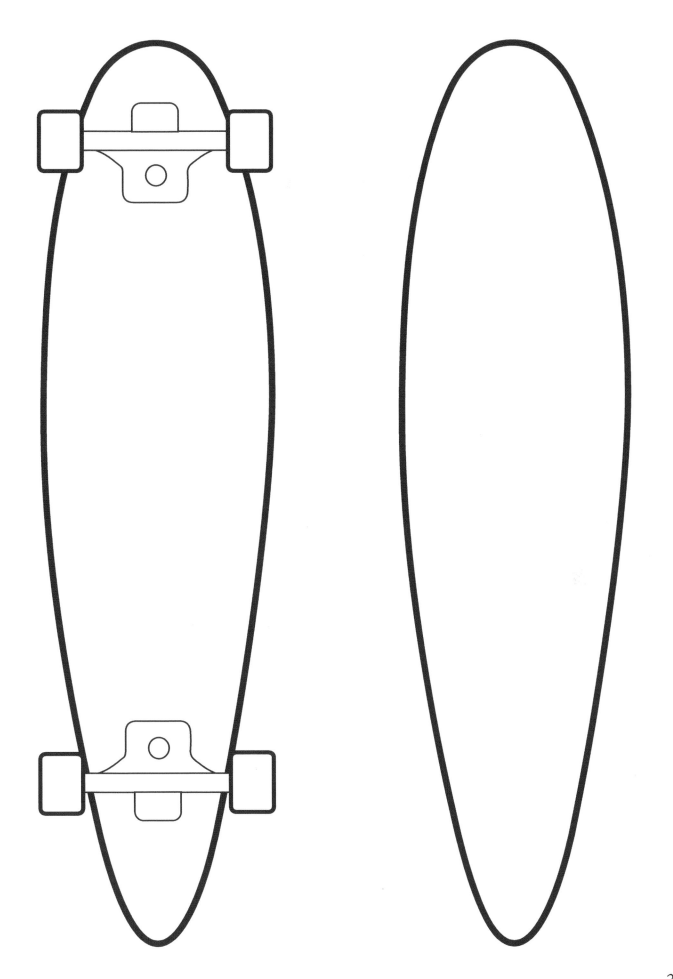

NAME OF BOARD:

DETAILS:

INSPIRATION:

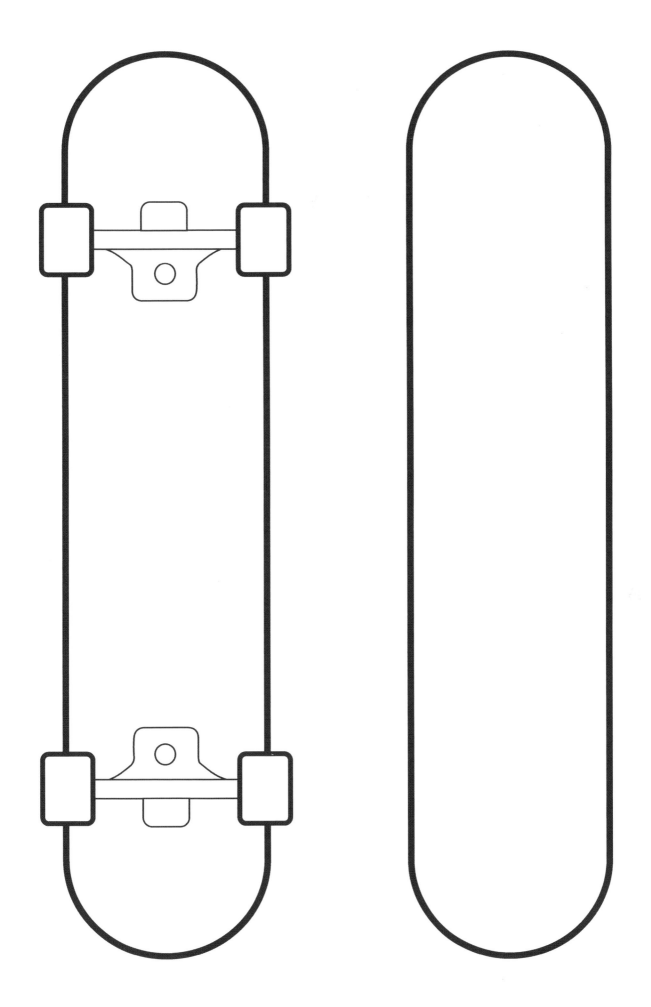

NAME OF BOARD:

DETAILS:

INSPIRATION:

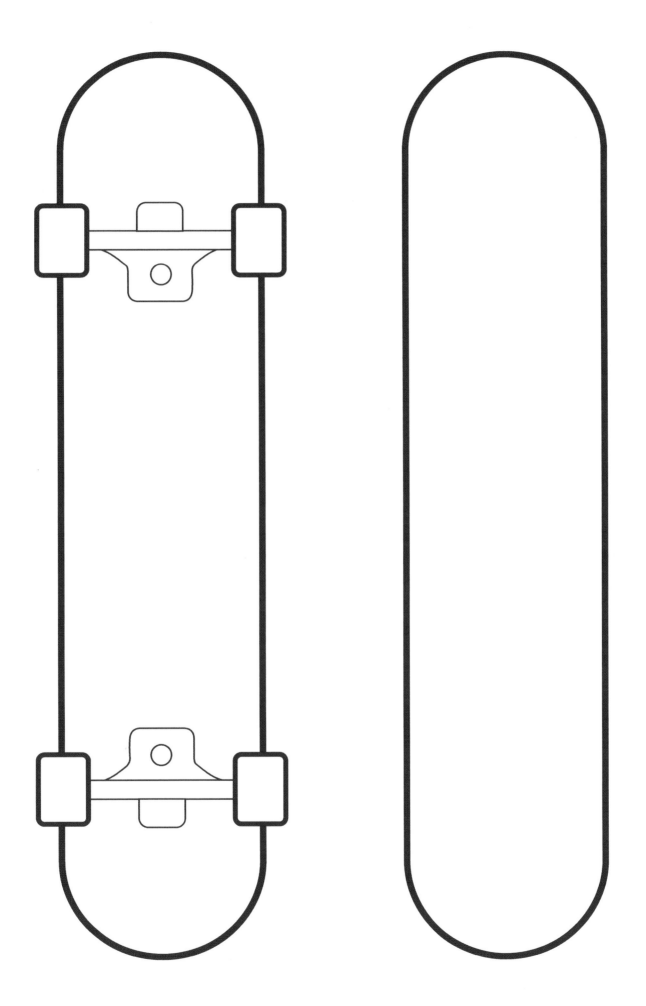

NAME OF BOARD:

DETAILS:

INSPIRATION:

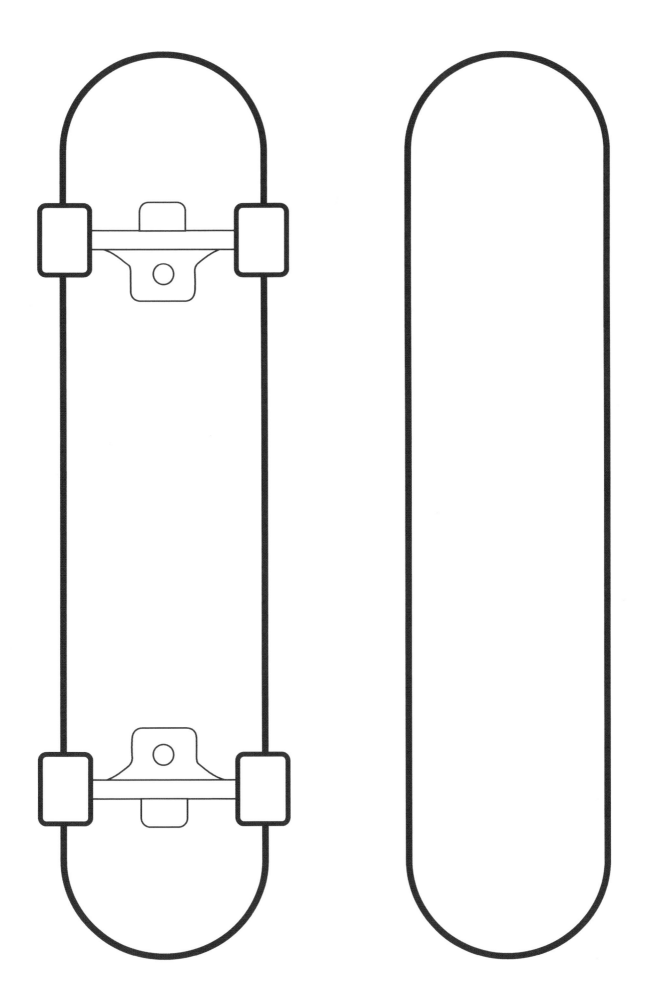

NAME OF BOARD:

DETAILS:

INSPIRATION:

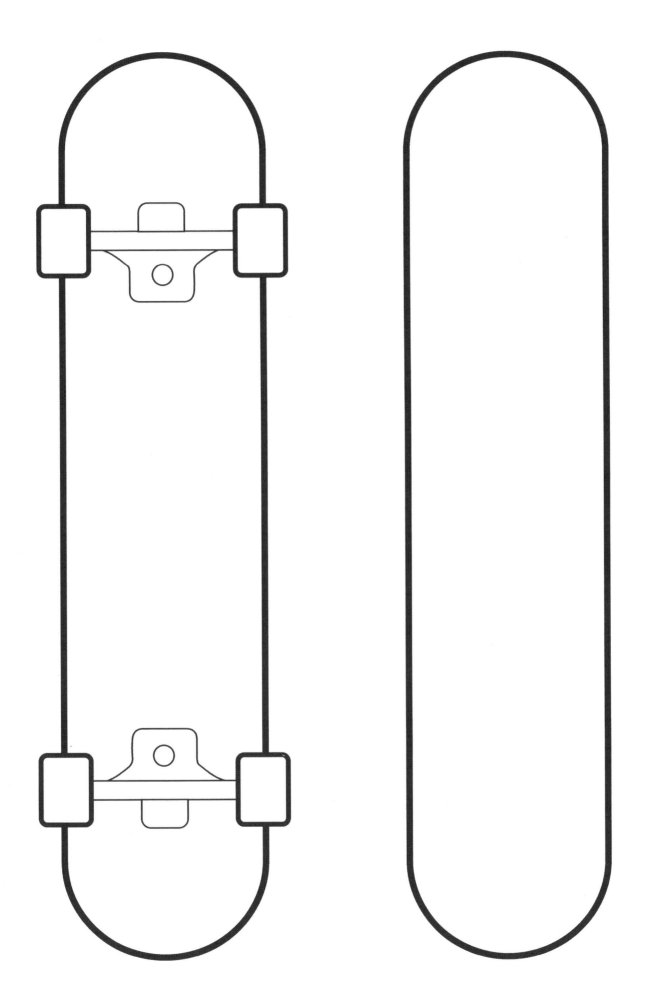

NAME OF BOARD:

DETAILS:

INSPIRATION:

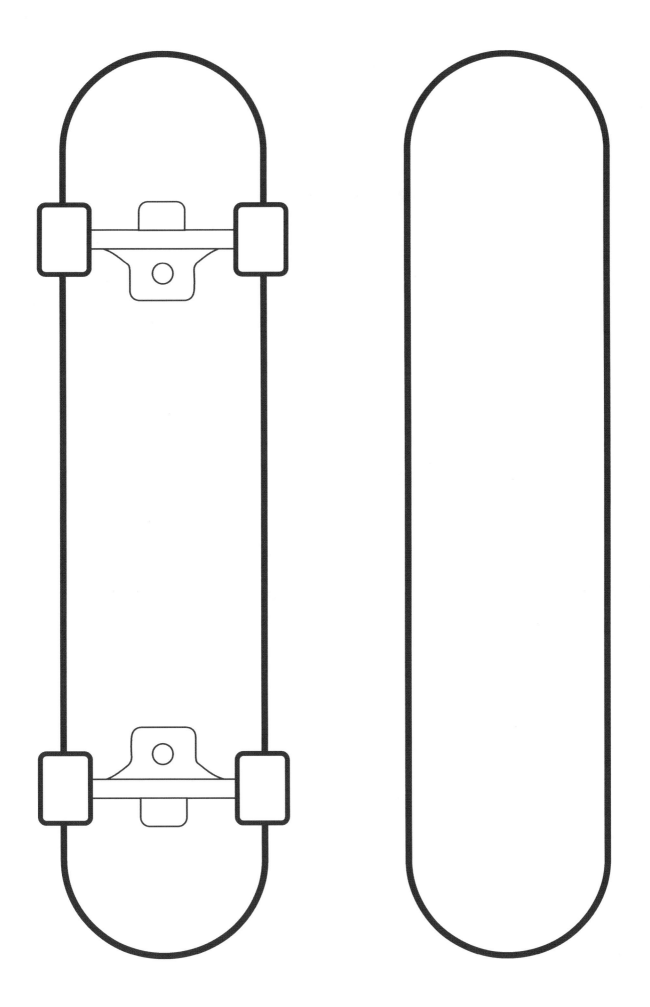

NAME OF BOARD:

DETAILS:

INSPIRATION:

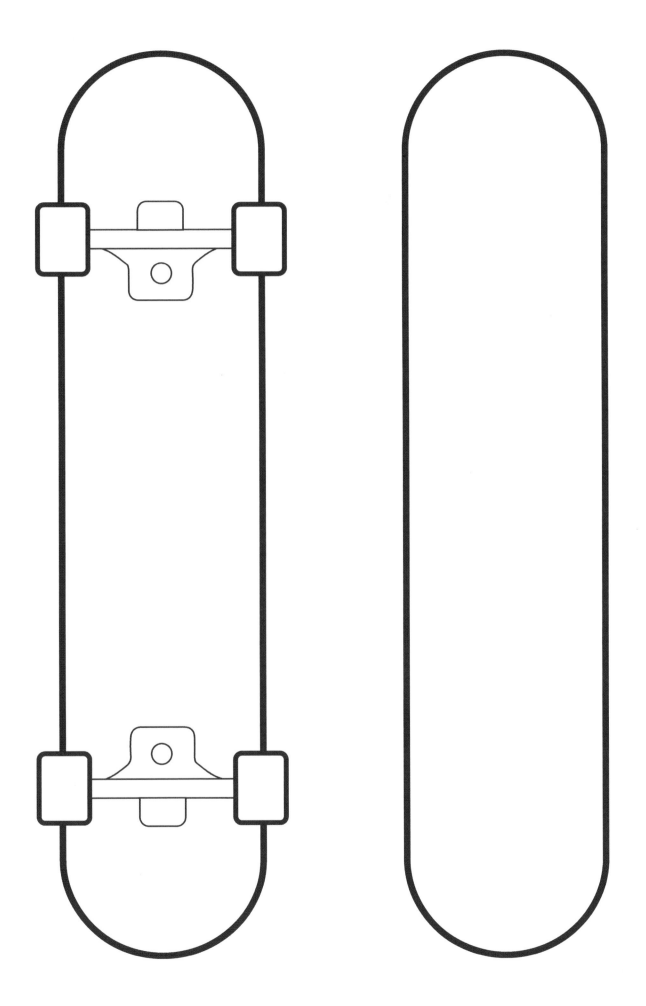

NAME OF BOARD:

DETAILS:

INSPIRATION:

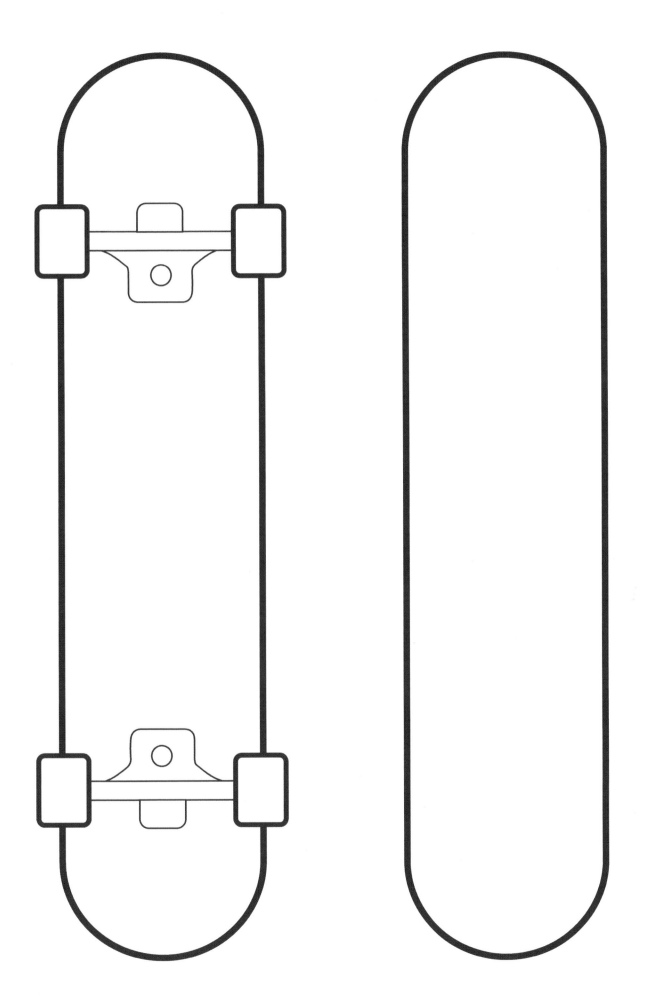

NAME OF BOARD:

DETAILS:

INSPIRATION:

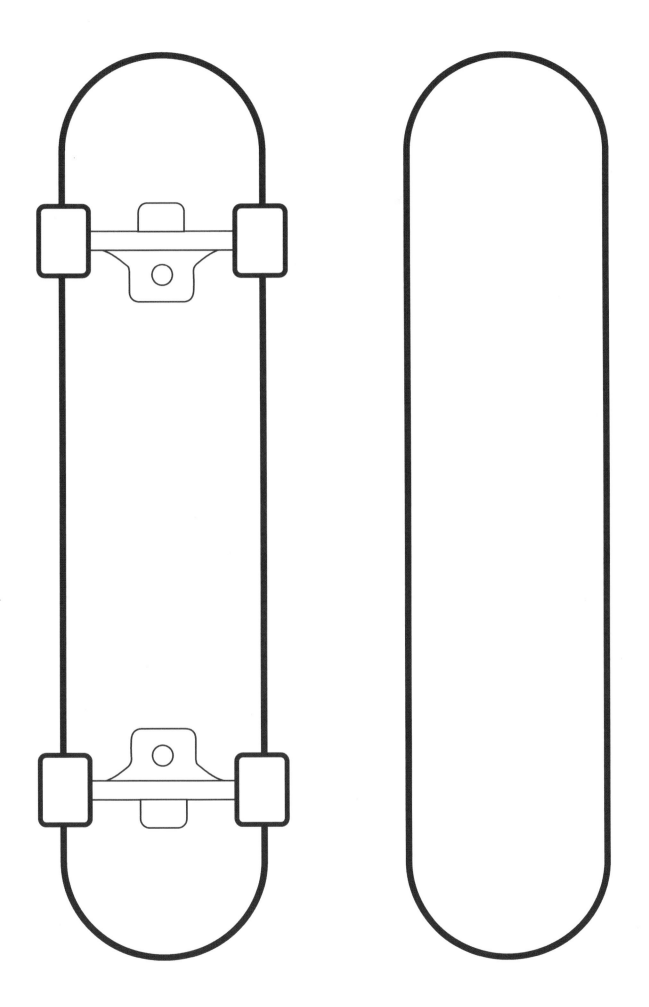

NAME OF BOARD:

DETAILS:

INSPIRATION:

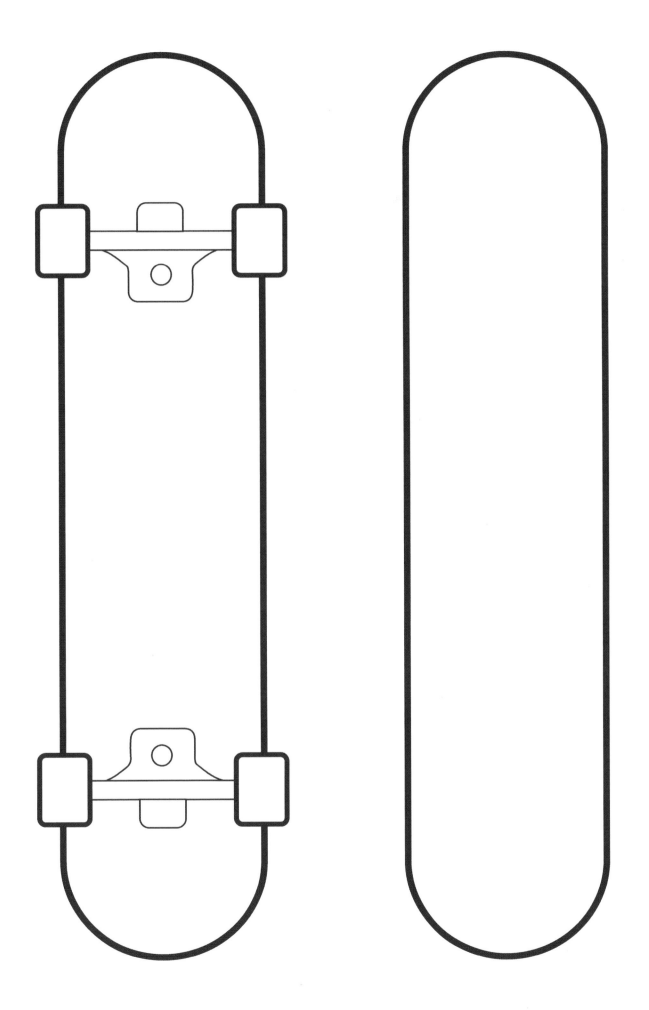

NAME OF BOARD:

DETAILS:

INSPIRATION:

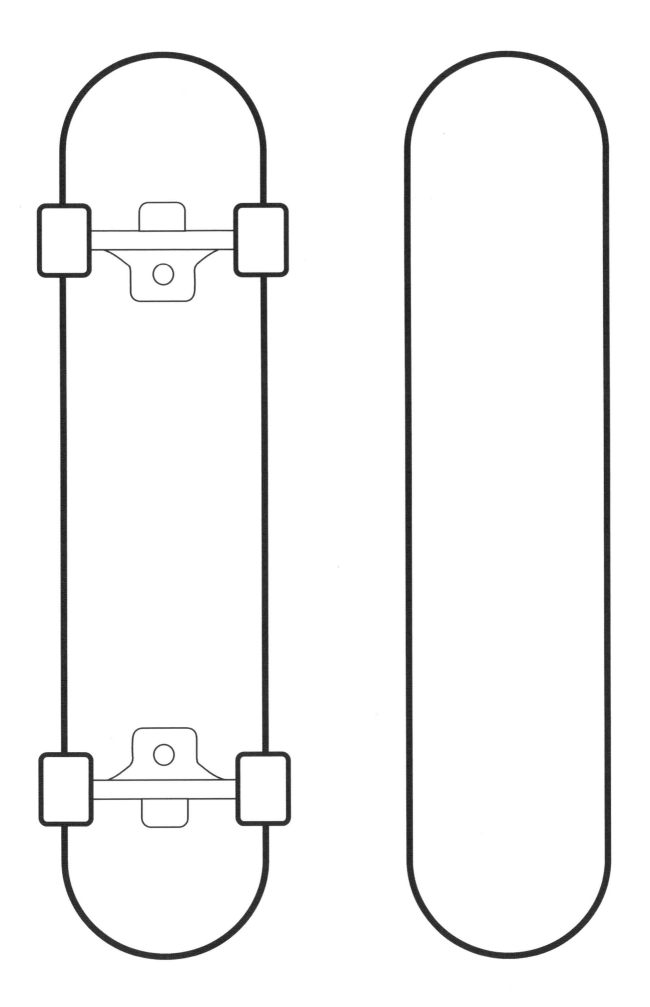

NAME OF BOARD:

DETAILS:

INSPIRATION:

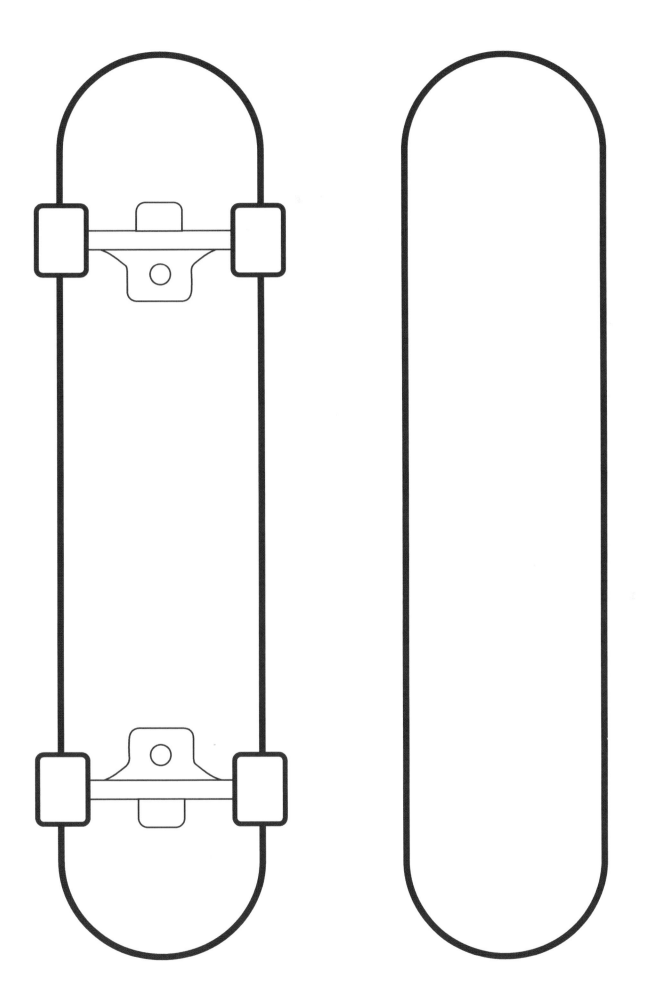

NAME OF BOARD:

DETAILS:

INSPIRATION:

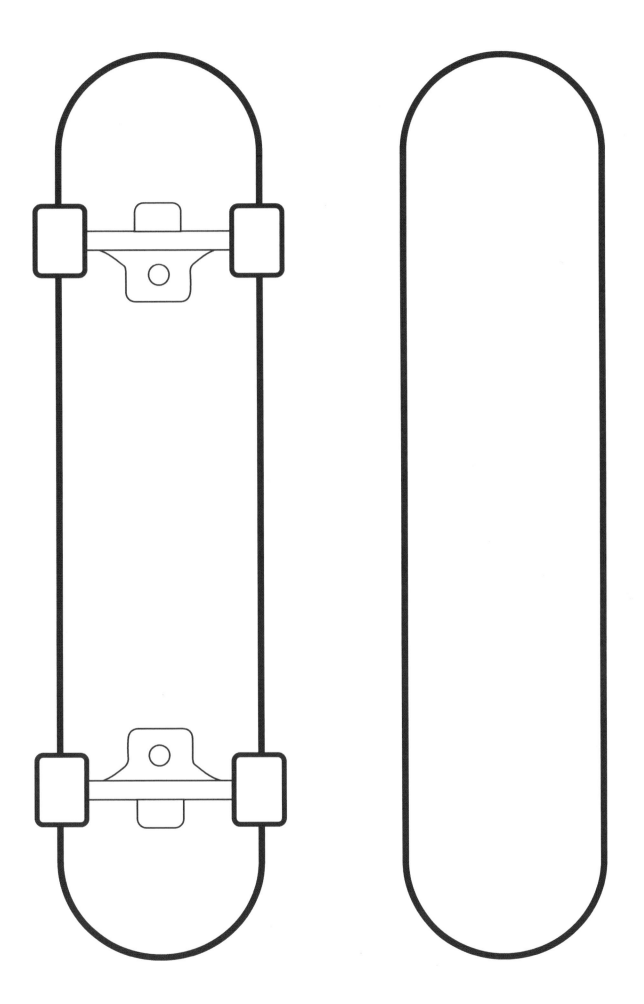

NAME OF BOARD:

DETAILS:

INSPIRATION:

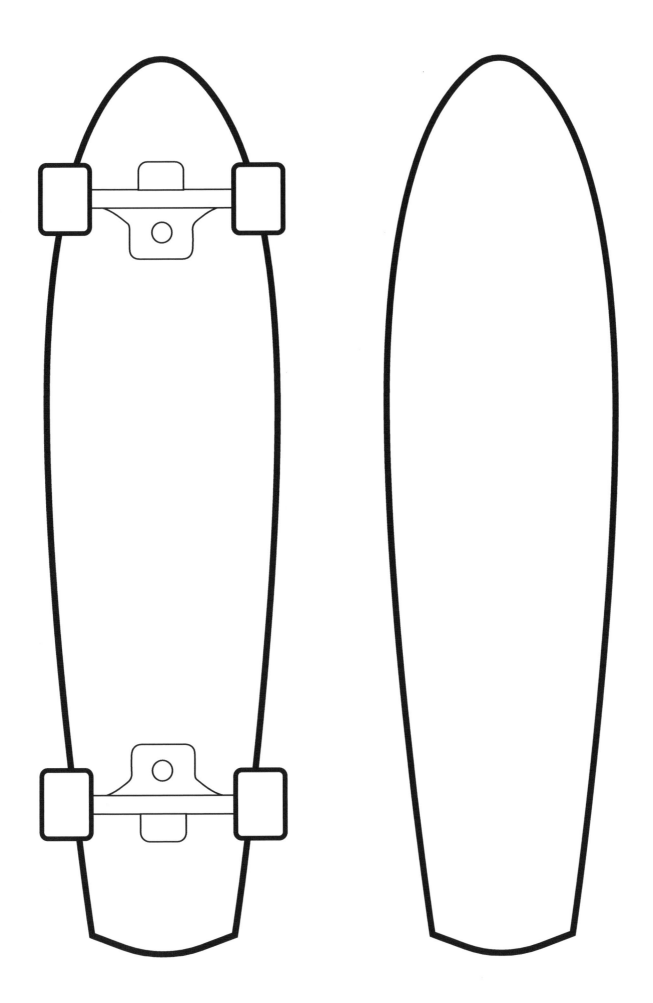

NAME OF BOARD:

DETAILS:

INSPIRATION:

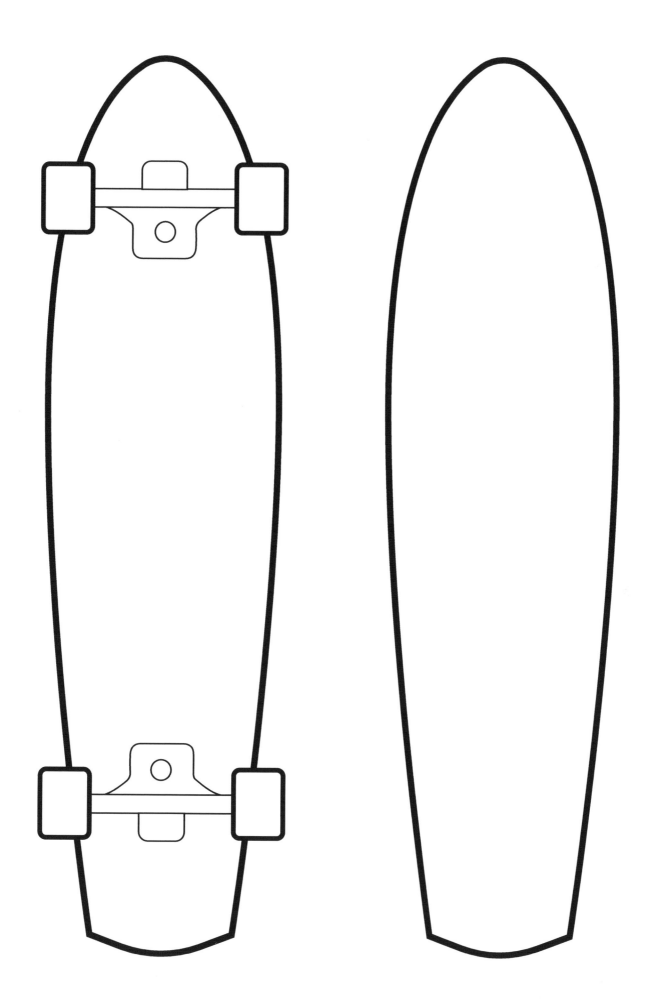

NAME OF BOARD:

DETAILS:

INSPIRATION:

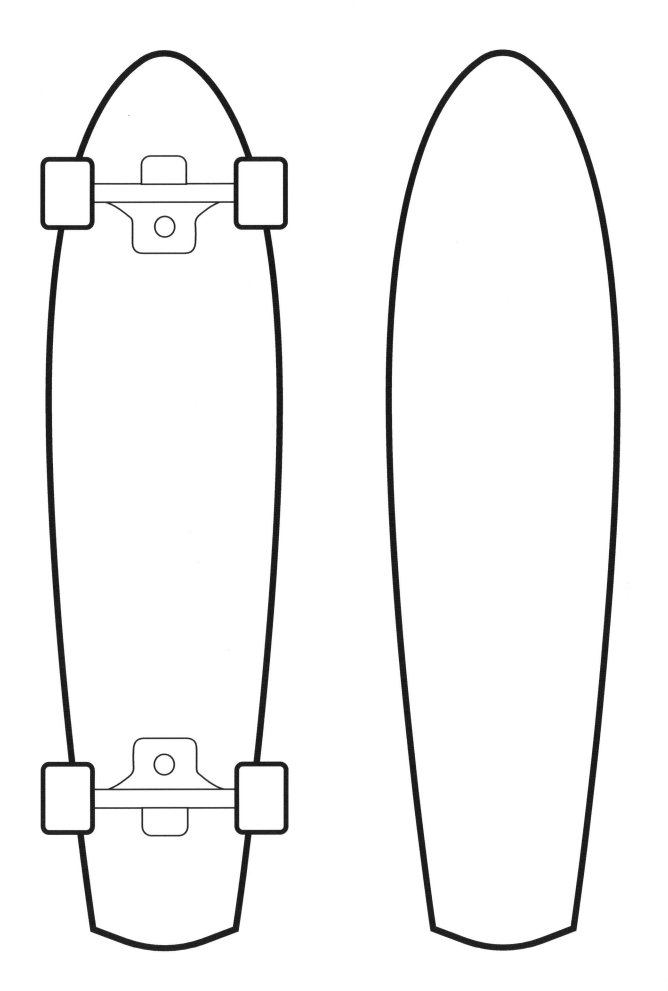

NAME OF BOARD:

DETAILS:

INSPIRATION:

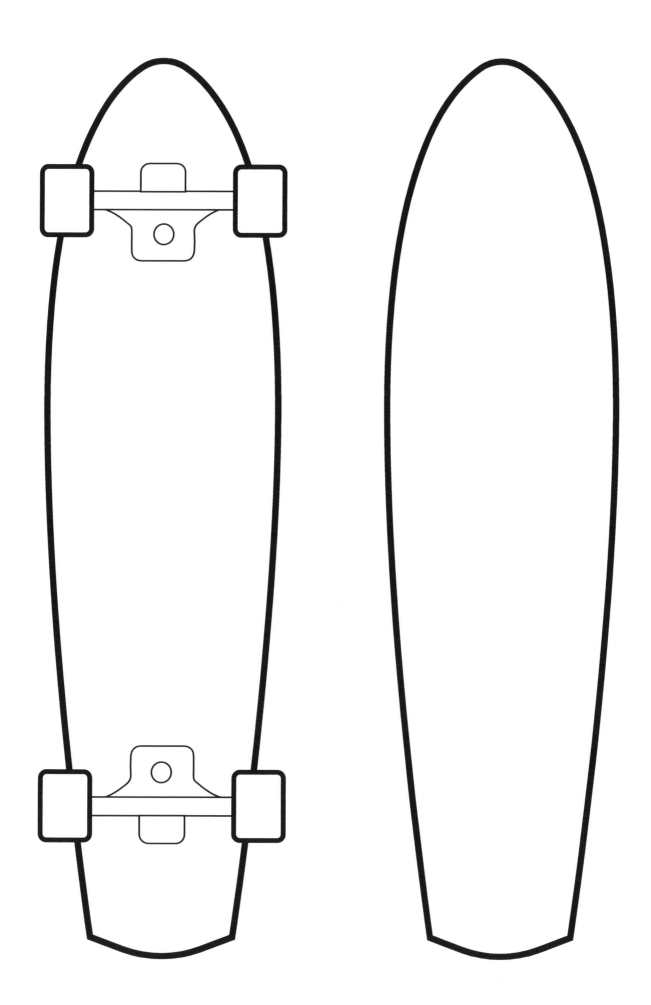

NAME OF BOARD:

DETAILS:

INSPIRATION:

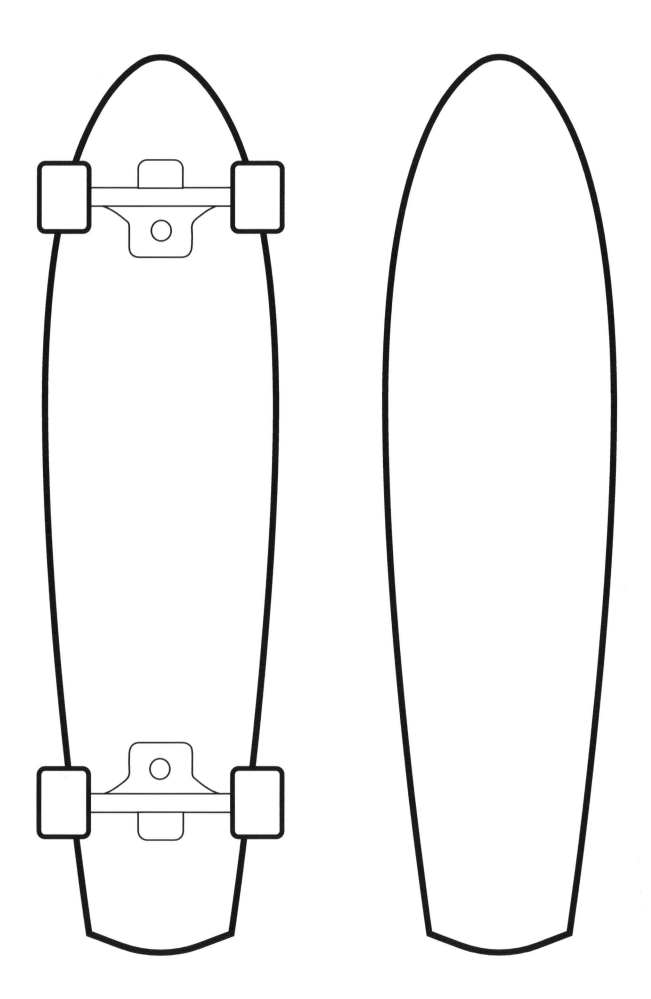

NAME OF BOARD:

DETAILS:

INSPIRATION:

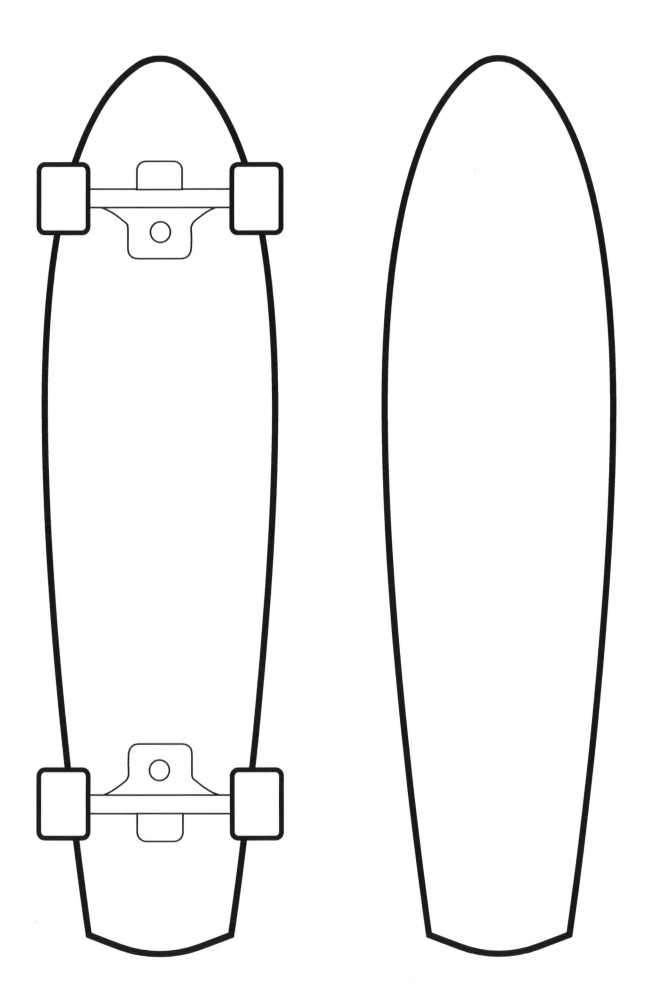

NAME OF BOARD:

DETAILS:

INSPIRATION:

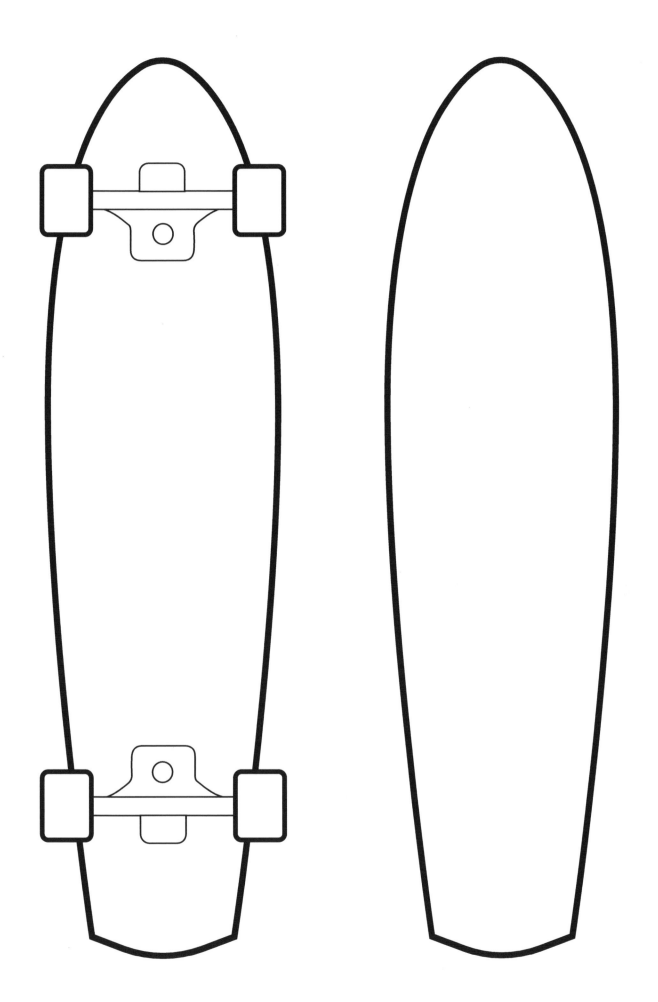

NAME OF BOARD:

DETAILS:

INSPIRATION:

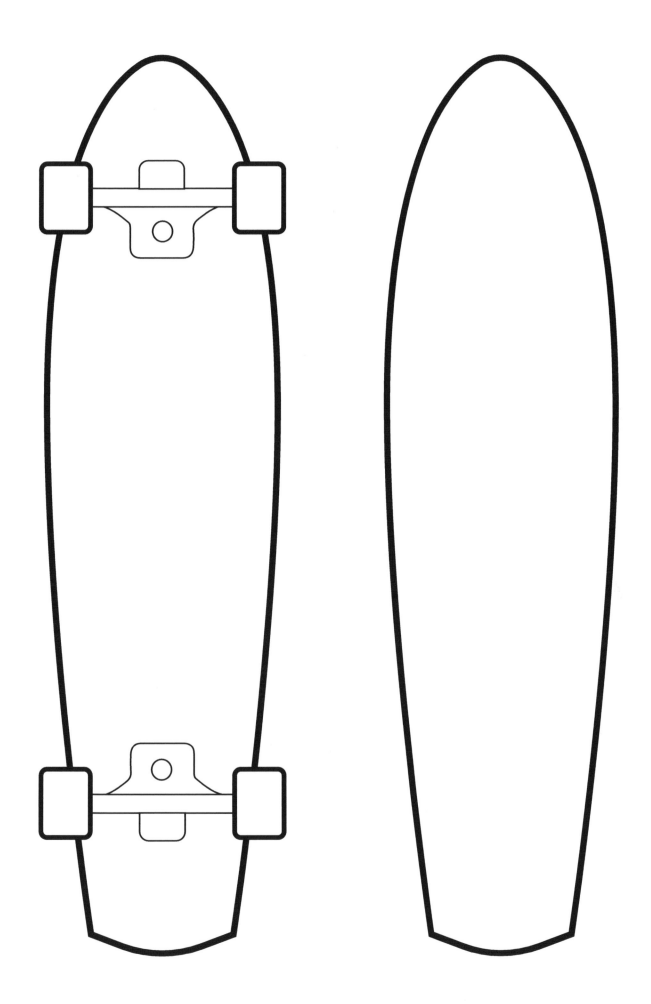

NAME OF BOARD:

DETAILS:

INSPIRATION:

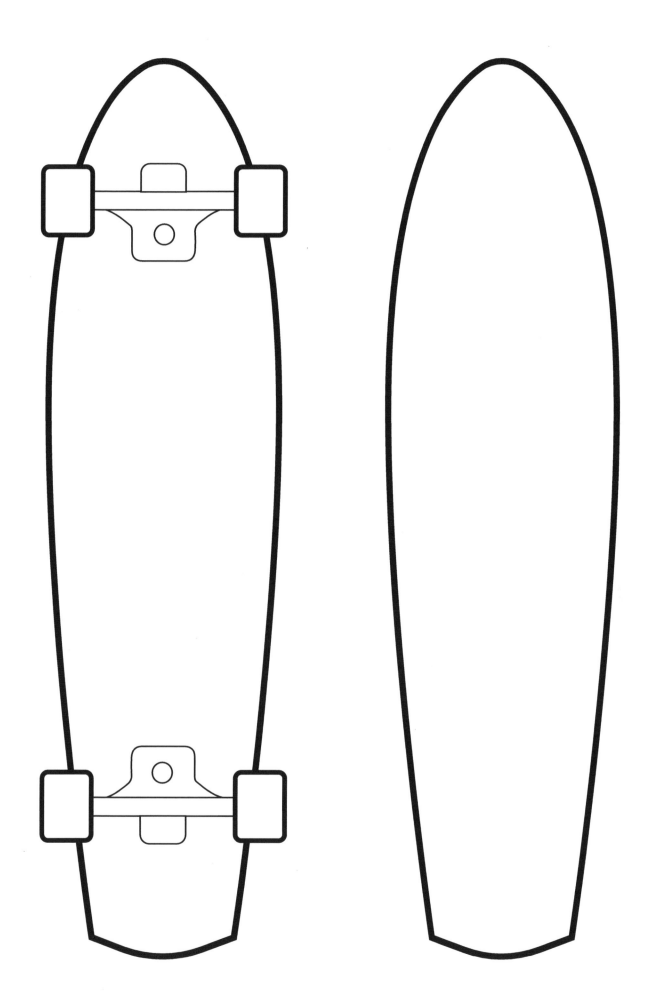

NAME OF BOARD:

DETAILS:

INSPIRATION:

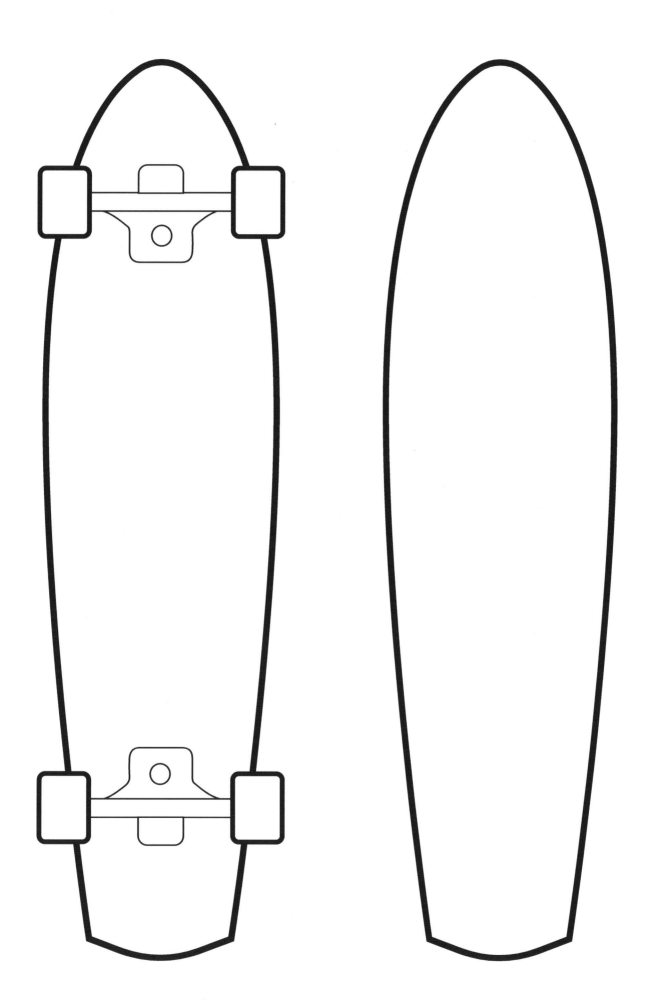

NAME OF BOARD:

DETAILS:

INSPIRATION:

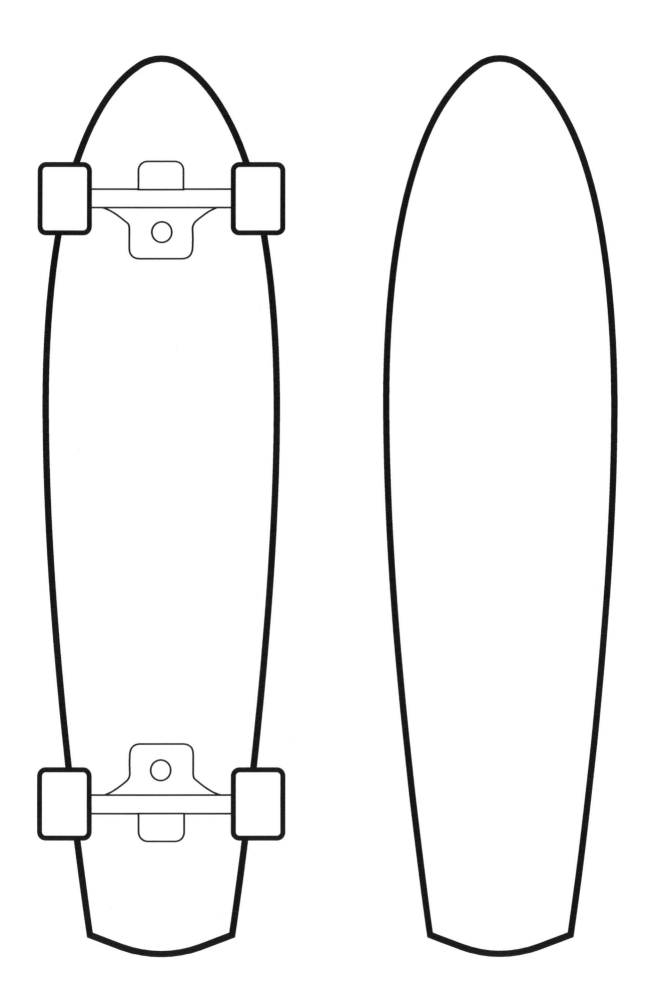

73

NAME OF BOARD:

DETAILS:

INSPIRATION:

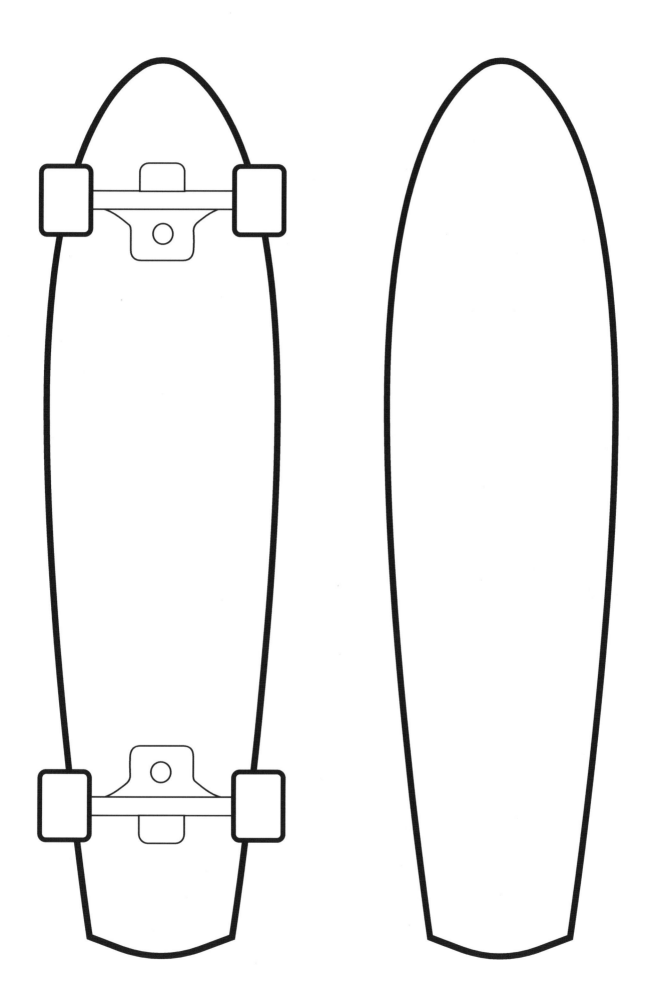

NAME OF BOARD:

DETAILS:

INSPIRATION:

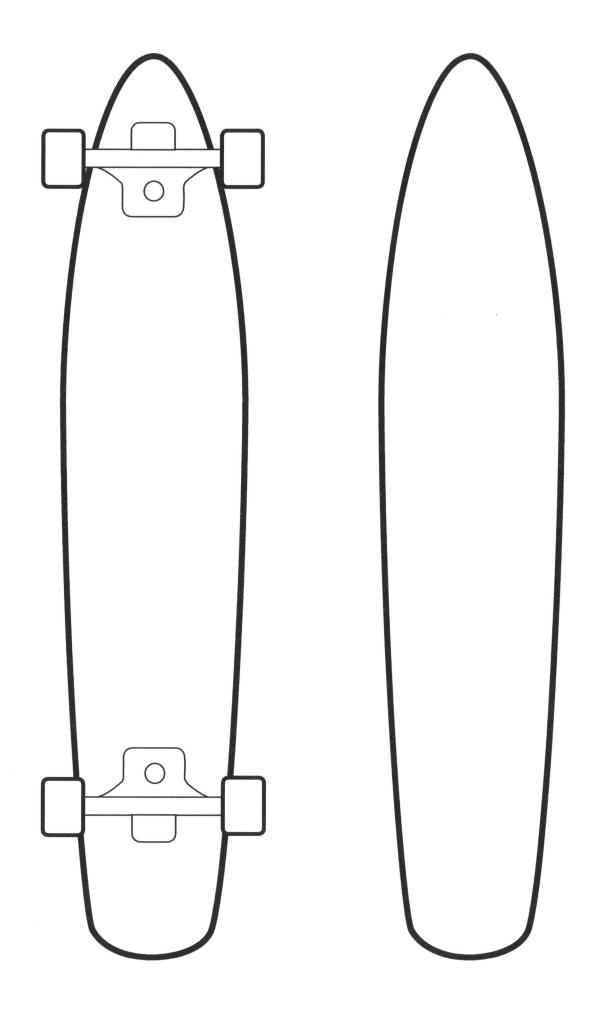

NAME OF BOARD:

DETAILS:

INSPIRATION:

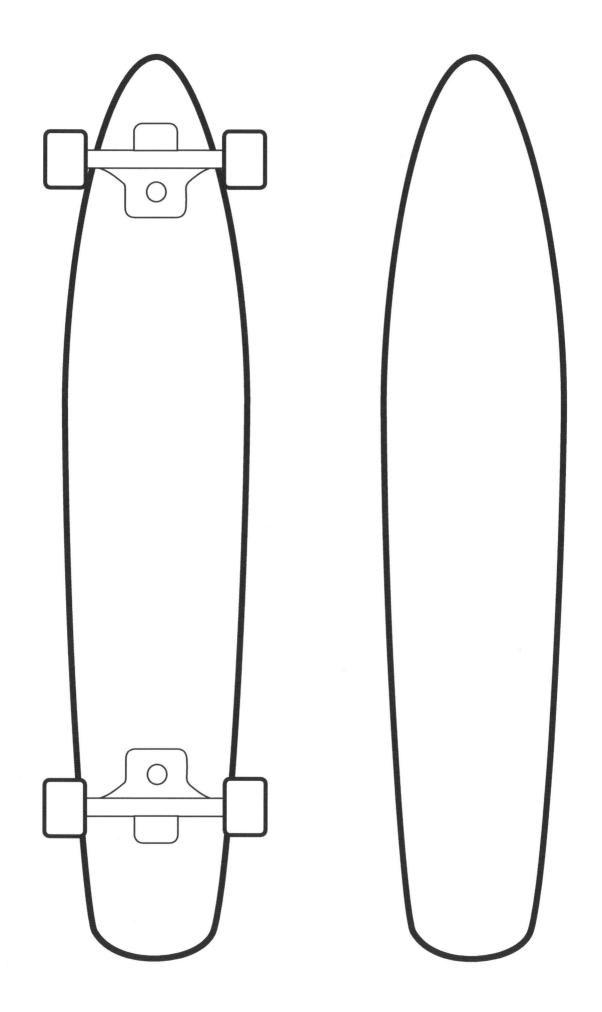

NAME OF BOARD:

DETAILS:

INSPIRATION:

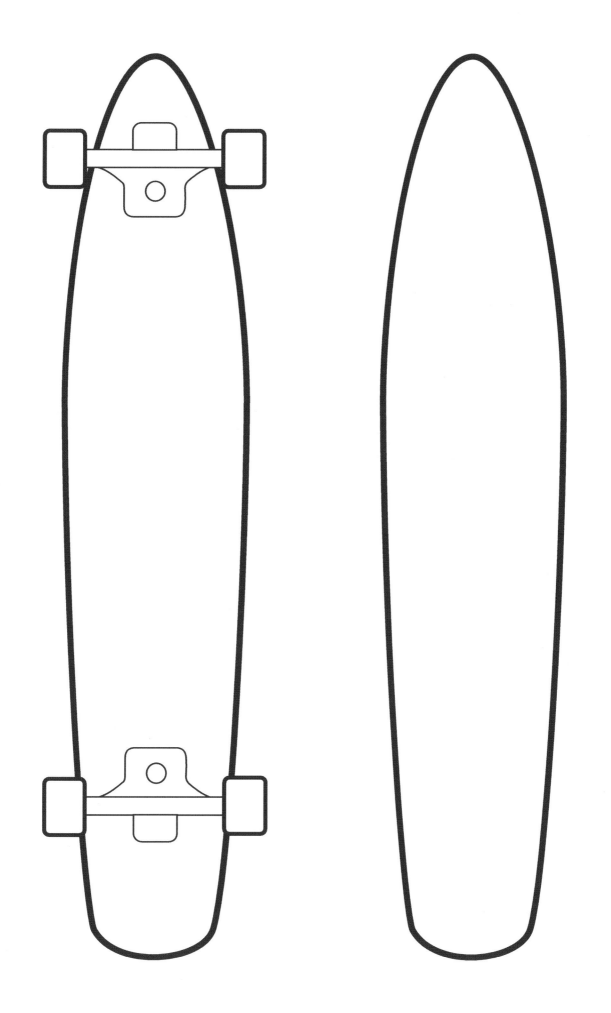

NAME OF BOARD:

DETAILS:

INSPIRATION:

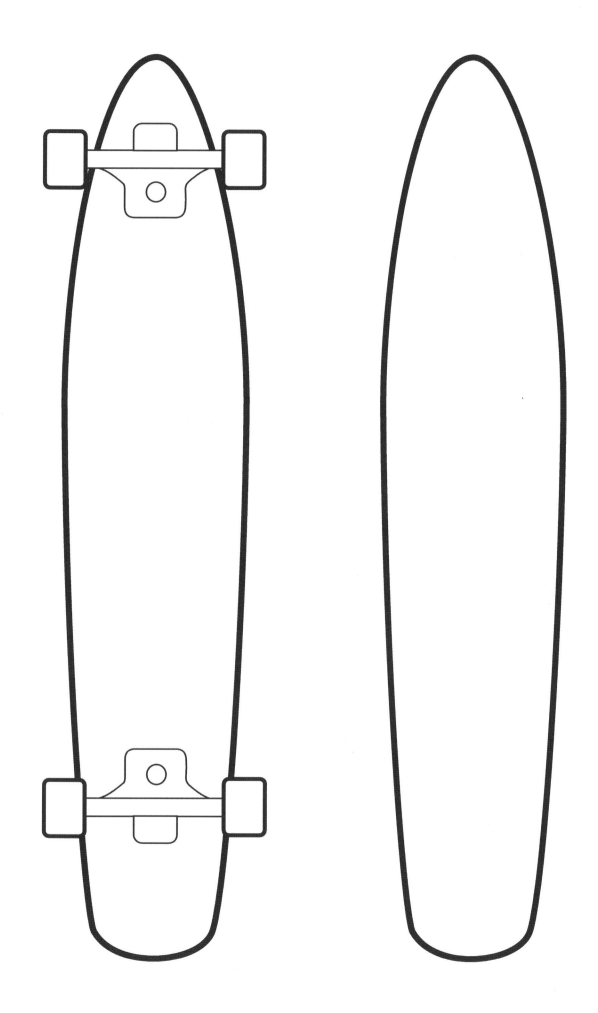

NAME OF BOARD:

DETAILS:

INSPIRATION:

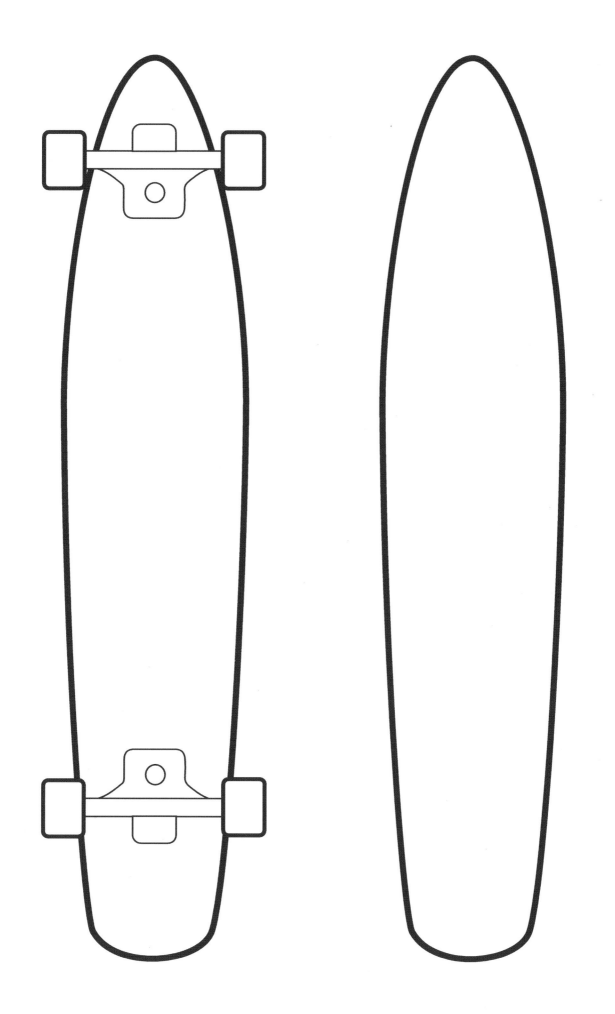

NAME OF BOARD:

DETAILS:

INSPIRATION:

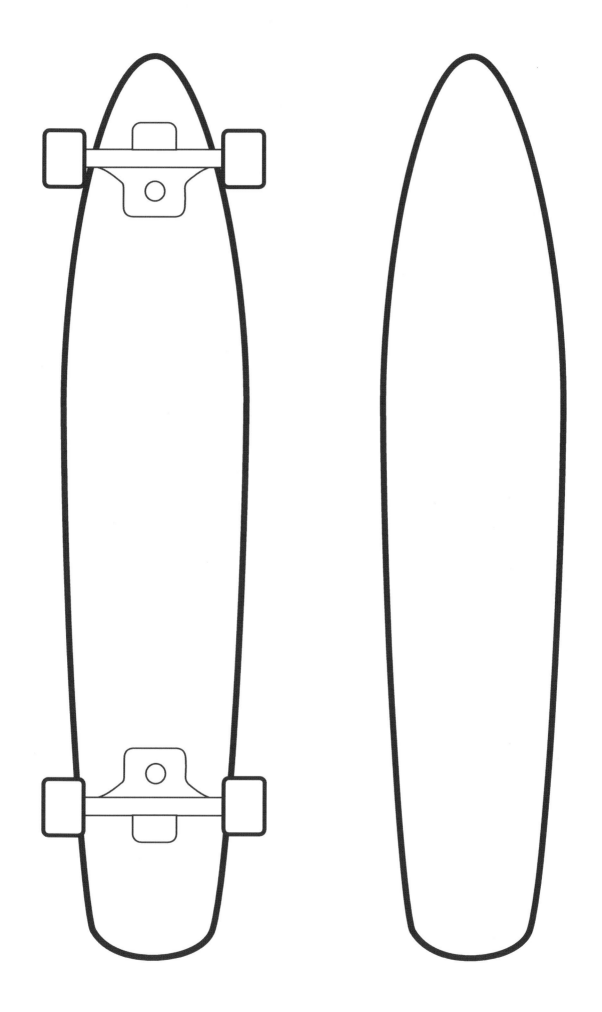

NAME OF BOARD:

DETAILS:

INSPIRATION:

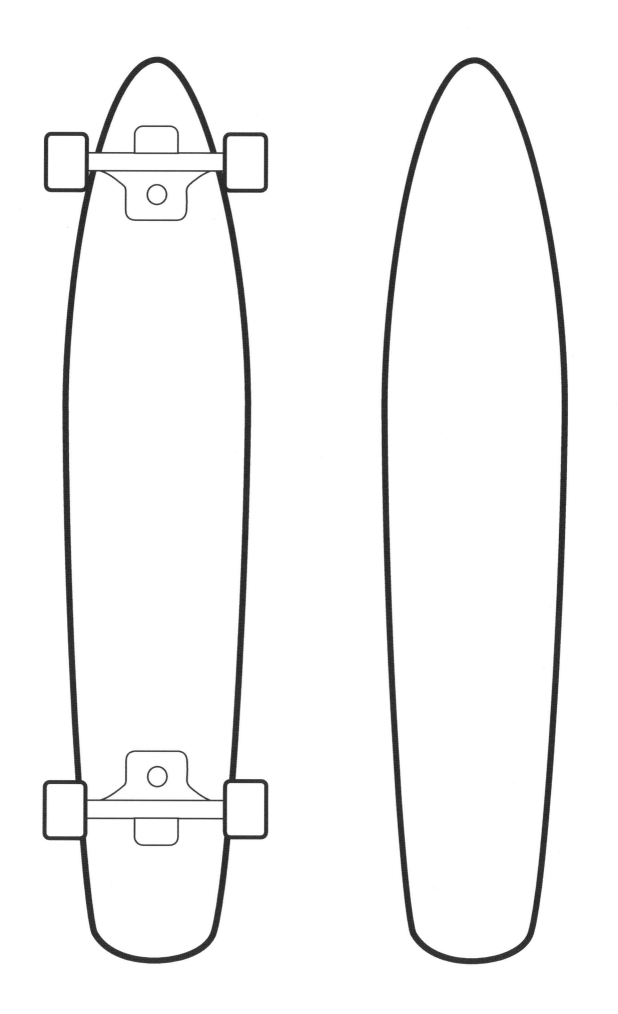

NAME OF BOARD:

DETAILS:

INSPIRATION:

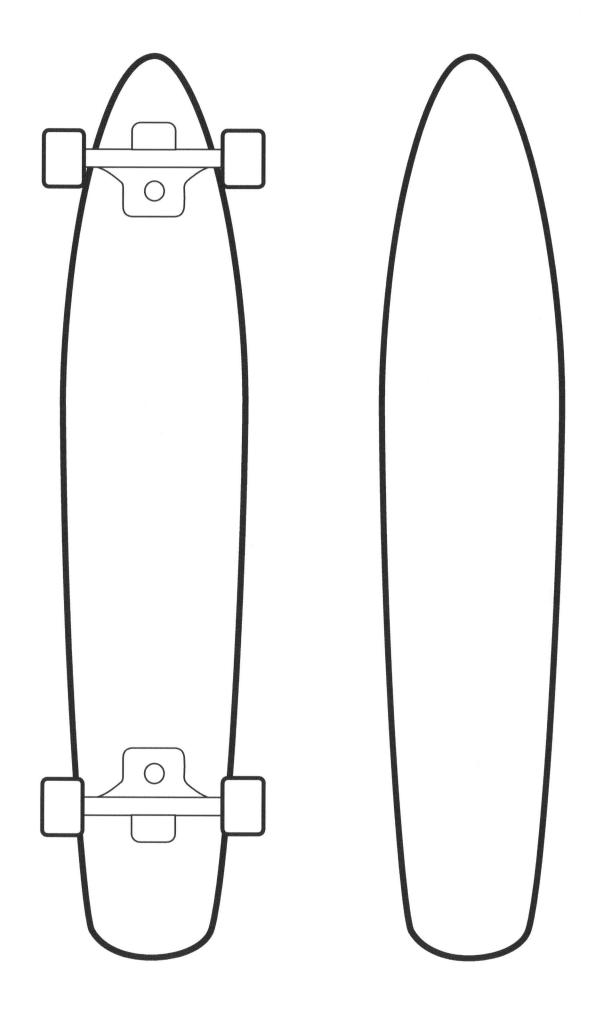

NAME OF BOARD:

DETAILS:

INSPIRATION:

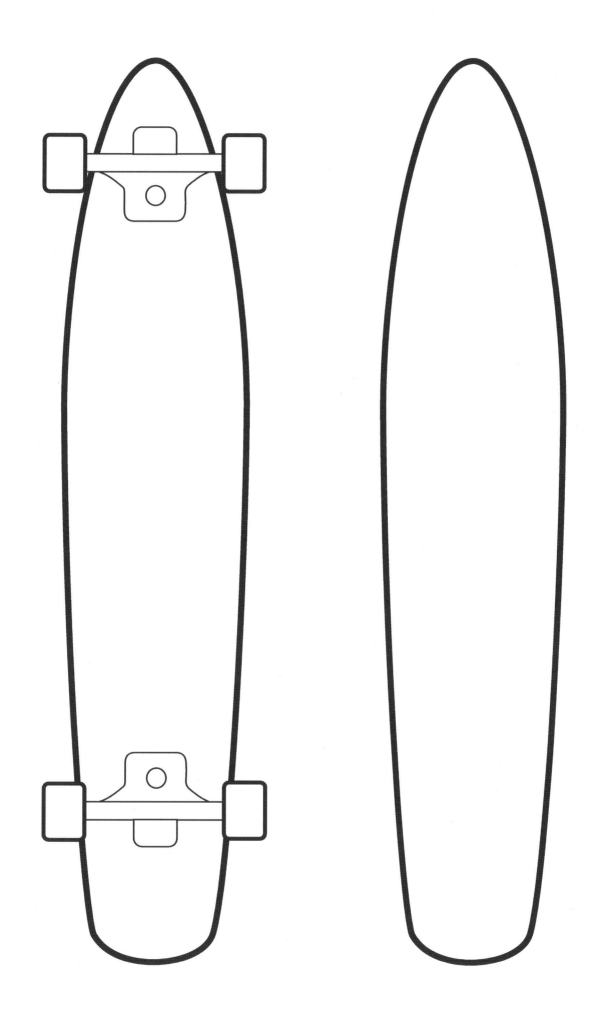

NAME OF BOARD:

DETAILS:

INSPIRATION:

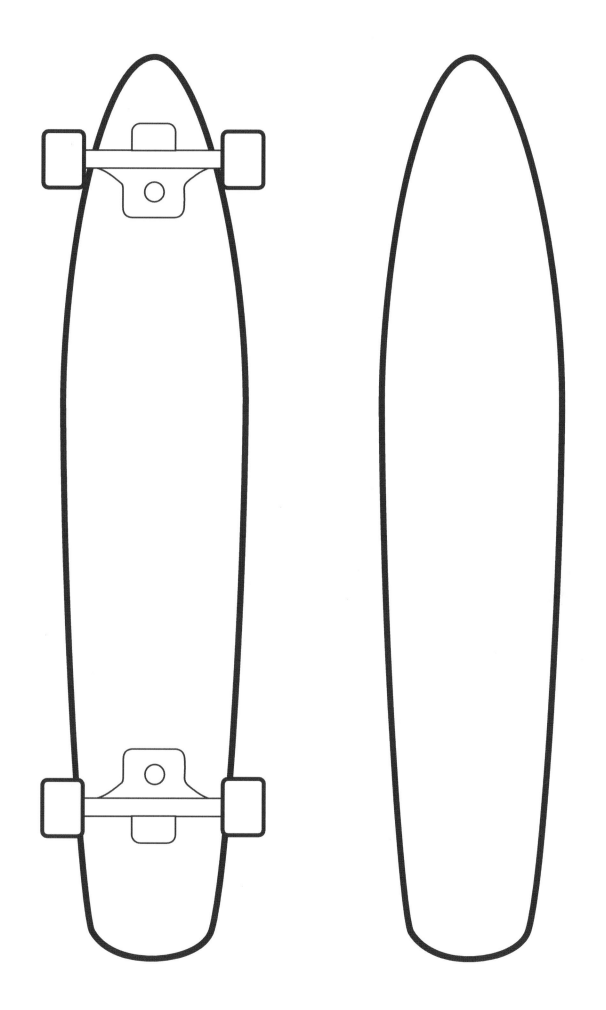

NAME OF BOARD:

DETAILS:

INSPIRATION:

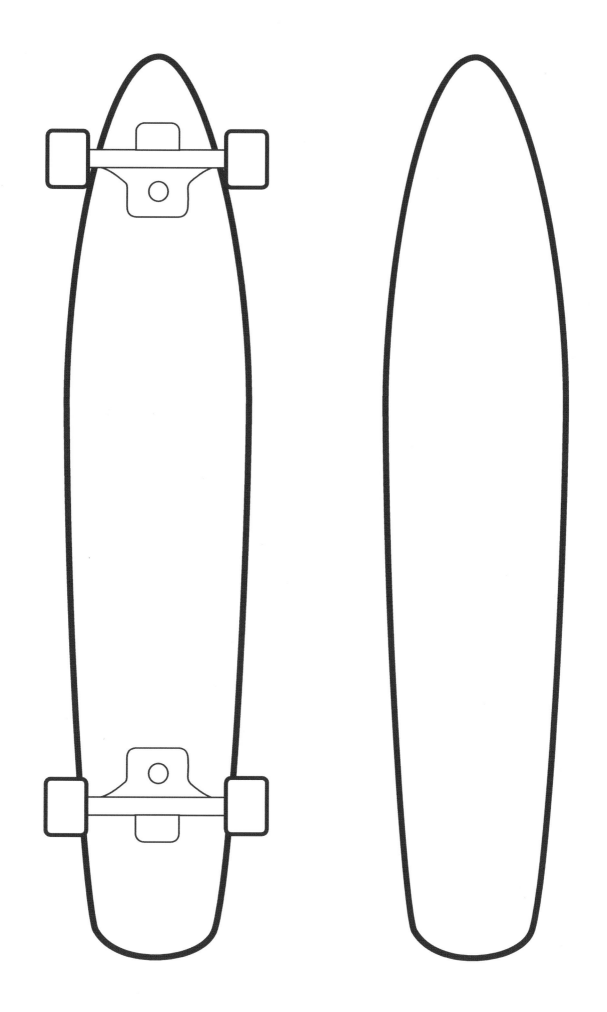

NAME OF BOARD:

DETAILS:

INSPIRATION:

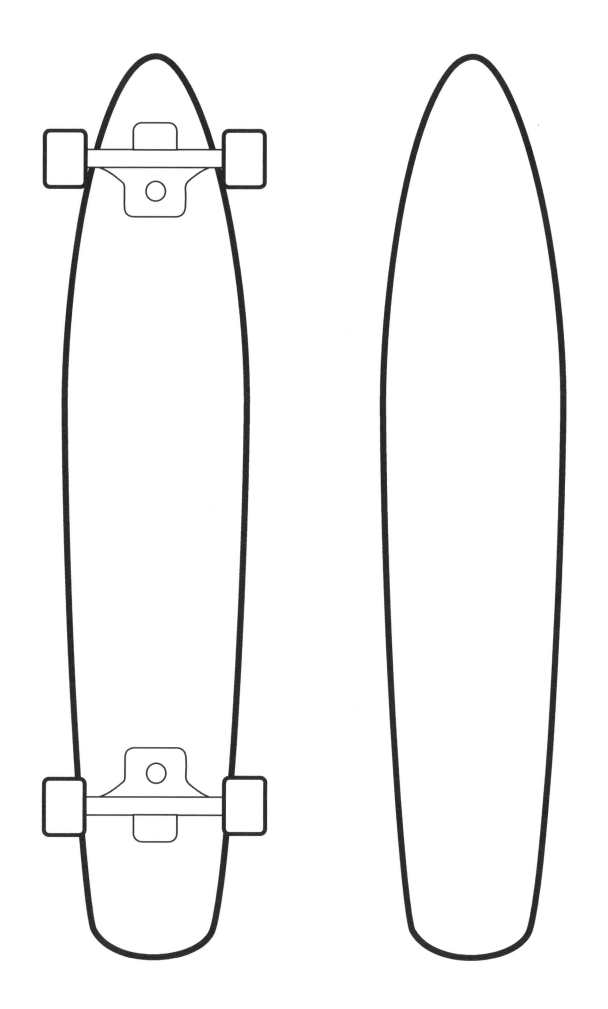

JUST SKATE

JOURNALS

sketchbooks, planners,
notebooks and journals
for skateboarders

surfskatecollective@gmail.com

PUBLISHED BY SURF SKATE COLLECTIVE

Printed in Great Britain
by Amazon